Cover *Naval Reserve F/A-18 Hornet;* **page 1** *Marine Corps Reserve F-4 Phantoms;* **pages 2-3** *Louisiana Air National Guard F-15 Eagle over New Orleans;* **pages 6-7** *Naval Reserve F-14 Tomcat followed by TOP GUN (Naval Fighter Weapons School) instructors in an F-5 and A-4;* **pages 8-9** *Virginia Army National Guard UH-60 Black Hawk ten feet above brush at 170 miles per hour;* **pages 10-11** *Air Force Reserve C-5 Galaxy taking off;* **pages 12-13** *Air Force Reserve A-10 Warthog over a bombing range in Mississippi.*

Marine Corps Reserve F-4

Published by Thomasson-Grant, Inc.: Frank L. Thomasson III
and John F. Grant, Directors; Megan R. Youngquist, Art Director;
Jim Gibson, Production Manager; Carolyn M. Clark, Senior Editor.
Designed by Leonard G. Phillips
Edited by Rebecca Beall Barns
Introduction by Barry Goldwater
Interviews by Jeffrey Ethell
Copyright © 1988 by Thomasson-Grant, Inc. All rights reserved.
Photographs copyright © 1988 by George Hall.
Photograph pages 44-45 copyright © 1988 by C.J. Heatley III.
Photograph page 50 copyright © 1988 by Jeffrey Ethell.
Illustrations courtesy of Pilot Press. A-3 illustration courtesy
of Arnoldo Mondadori Editore, S.p.A., Milano,
and The Military Press, distributed by Crown Publishers, 1983.
This book, or any portions thereof, may not be reproduced in any form
without written permission of the publisher, Thomasson-Grant, Inc.
Library of Congress Catalog Card Number: 87-40600
ISBN 0-934738-33-5
Printed and bound in Japan by Dai Nippon Printing Co., Ltd.

95 94 93 92 91 90 89 88   5 4 3 2 1

Any inquiries should be directed to the publisher, Thomasson-Grant, Inc.,
One Morton Drive, Suite 500, Charlottesville, Virginia 22901,
telephone (804) 977-1780.

THOMASSON-GRANT

TOTAL FORCE

FLYING WITH AMERICA'S RESERVE AND GUARD

PHOTOGRAPHY BY GEORGE HALL

INTRODUCTION BY BARRY GOLDWATER

INTERVIEWS BY JEFFREY ETHELL

EVEN BEFORE THE AMERICAN REVOLUTION, the colonists had a concept of total force. Minutemen fought side by side with the militia in skirmishes with the British. Today the National Guard and Reserve augment the Army, Navy, Air Force, and Marines, forming a crucial part of the organization of our armed forces.

My deep interest in the Reserve and Guard is based on experience. I've been an officer in the Air Force and Army Reserves for almost 40 years, a pilot for nearly 60. When my college roommate suggested we join the Air Corps together, I thought that was an excellent idea because I already had my private pilot's license. But the Corps rejected me because I couldn't read the eye chart.

I came on duty as a reserve first lieutenant of the infantry, still determined to fly. In 1932, I applied to become an Air Corps cadet, but my vision hadn't improved, and at the age of 23 I was too old. I secured active pilot status in World War II, but wasn't allowed to fly in combat, which really frustrated me. In addition to my age, the fact that I didn't have Air Corps training was against me, because men were required to learn basic skills with the Corps to understand things like flying in formation, something never needed when piloting private planes.

Facing Arizona Air National Guard F-16B refueling from a KC-135; **above** fin flash on an Arizona Air National Guard A-7.

After training cadets in aerial gunnery in Arizona, I transferred to Air Transport Command and was assigned to the Second Ferrying Group in Delaware, a new classification of overage pilots organized to fly aircraft and supplies to war zones. In 17 months, our group flew virtually everything in the United States inventory, including the first single-seat P-47 Thunderbolts, high-performance fighters designed to protect our bombers. We ferried nine of these to Newfoundland, on to Greenland, Iceland, and finally to northern Scotland. Other assignments took us to North Africa, Burma, India, and over the Himalayan Hump into China.

In those days, we didn't have the electronics that now enable a pilot to fly anywhere, anytime. By day the navigator on board plotted and checked our course by observing the sun. By night we kept our heading and prayed that the sun would be out the next morning so the navigator could take a shot

Within range of shore, our automatic direction equipment pointed a needle where we wanted to go. When turning the aircraft, we made sure we kept the needle in the center. We had to be careful because the Germans, who had a station on the tip of Norway just a few degrees off the heading for Scotland, sent up false ADF [automatic direction finder] signals. I lost several good friends who went the wrong way.

Today everything is automatic. A pilot who wants to can let the system land the aircraft for him. In a flight from Phoenix to England, an automatic navigation system can take an aircraft to within 50 feet of the runway. But few pilots like automatic landings; they want to have that stick in their hands. The last thing a pilot will do is give up control of a plane.

When I returned from World War II, the Governor of Arizona asked me to organize a state Air National Guard unit, which I proceeded to do in 1946 with the help of young officers who had just come back from the war. Some of the men still serving in the Arizona Air National Guard were put on duty 40 years ago when I was in charge.

Washington Air National Guard KC-135 refueling an F-4 with F-106s overhead; **facing** *Arizona Air National Guard F-16 instructor Lt. Col. Bob "Cass" Cassaro.*

The men who have stayed with the Reserve and Guard have seen many changes. When I first became an officer, servicemen in the regular forces barely put up with reservists. Instructors transferred to the National Guard were usually fellows with bad records who were sent to us as a last resort. Now things are entirely different; officers assigned to the Reserve and Guard take great pride in their work. The quality of training for the reserves is as good as that for the regular service.

There's a clear, new-found sense of purpose in the Reserve and Guard. Better chances for promotion and better retirement pay have attracted motivated, well-qualified applicants. Where once as few as a dozen people might participate in a drill in Arizona, now a whole outfit turns up with pride.

When the Arizona Air National Guard was first organized, the military assigned us more old planes than new. We weren't kept abreast of innovations. Only in the past 20 years have the reserves received more modern equipment. We have a somewhat dated but very active KC-135 tanker outfit in Arizona that supplies fuel for bombers and fighters. A number of new F-16s have recently been added to the state's inventory.

As a result of these improvements, every reserve unit plays a vital role in the defense of the United States. In World War II, less than ten percent of military officers came from West Point and the Naval Academy. The rest came from ROTC and Officers' Candidate School. The academies can't produce the number of men needed in a major conflict. The regular services can rely, though, on the Arizona National Guard's tanker group, the Colorado National Guard's fighter outfit, or any other carefully trained unit to integrate with regular forces within 24 hours.

A man in the Reserve or National Guard drills at least once a month and participates in a two-week summer maneuver. In addition to the skills reinforced in practice exercises, a number of men in the reserves contribute an enormous amount of practical military experience gained in Korea and Vietnam. When it comes down to it, these men have longer and more thorough training than most in the regular forces.

The military tries to give all active servicemen in the Navy, Air Force, Army, and Marines at least 20 hours flying time a month. Some Guardsmen and Reservists in Arizona get as many as 60 hours. Many reserve pilots have more than 7,000 hours flying time on record, while few men in regular outfits ever exceed 3,000 hours. Attracted by excellent opportunities for flight time as well as good equipment, many men sign on with the Air Reserve and Air National Guard. The Army attracts fewer men, especially in states like Arizona where exercises take place in searing heat.

Routine drills and maneuvers establish significant bonds between officers and their men. I think it is important that units be called into action, not just individuals. Men who train together in an artillery outfit work much better in the field with their colleagues than they will standing next to strangers. There is great strength in knowing what your wingman's going to do, in knowing what your maintenance people can do. Such strength is essential to the security of the United States.

Some people stress cost-effectiveness as a major reason for expanding the Reserve and National Guard, but cost-effectiveness is a misunderstood and overused expression. Training men in the Arizona Air National Guard is less expensive than training regular forces because we don't have a high turnover. We can take care of wasteful spending, but I don't think we can develop fighting units for our country based on economy. We must support these forces on their own merits as our best defense. Present a solid front to the enemy, and he will leave you alone. That is _real_ cost-effectiveness.

In a sense, the total force of this country includes all the people of the United States. I think it's a shortcoming that so few citizens have ever served in the armed forces. In times of peace, a man can fulfill an obligation to his country in the Guard or Reserve without spending too much time away from home or work.

Forty years' experience in the reserves has been invaluable to me in the Senate. I gained intimate knowledge of tactics, strategy, and acquisition. As Chairman of the Armed Services Committee, I could usually tell whether Congressional testimony was weak or strong. When I first worked on the Committee, almost all the members had been in the military; when I was in charge, only eight out of nineteen had ever worn a uniform. Even fewer Senators had flown in the services. When John Glenn and I talked about aircraft, the rest of the Senate listened.

I've flown the U-2, its successor the SR-71, the B-1 — in all 170 different aircraft. Even when I didn't get enough flight time to check out to fly a plane myself, I had a chance to go up in it, and I could talk about it. When people criticized the B-1, I had been in one, and I knew exactly what experts were talking about. When I flew the U-2, I sat in the back seat, observing takeoff, climb, and level flight. The fragile U-2 would only handle about three G forces, and that's not much. In the F-16, by comparison, I've pulled more than nine Gs. If I did that now, I'd fall apart.

People often ask me why I still fly. They might as well ask a man why he plays chess. Thinking through a problem while I'm flying clears my mind. I also get satisfaction from knowing what to do, how to do it, and when to do it. When I asked my wife to marry me, she said she would if I quit flying and learned how to play bridge. I never did either one.

The biggest reward I've had from flying isn't the close calls or interesting missions. The greatest thing is the comradeship of the people you know from 40 years ago. When you train young pilots, they remain your friends forever.

— BARRY GOLDWATER

Facing Alabama Air National Guard F-4 Phantom.

FIGHTER/ATTACK

Pages 20-21 *Louisiana Air National Guard F-15 Eagle;* **pages 22-23** *Naval Reserve F/A-18 Hornet;* **above** *Cdr. Scott "Mongoose" Davis in a Naval Reserve F/A-18.*

Digital panel and head-up display of an F/A-18; **pages 26-27** *Naval Reserve F/A-18.*

IN THE HORNET, everything is at your fingertips, either on the throttle or stick, to control radar, air-to-air missiles, and guns. The complex sensors in the F/A-18 identify airborne threats and help the pilot prioritize them, calculate whether the odds against him are overwhelming, or whether he can make it to a target and defend himself on the way out. Computers optimize the flight controls for whatever regime you are in, from slow speed to supersonic flight.

The difficult thing about the F/A-18 is keeping up with the options. It's a challenge to draw on all the available information and use it wisely and efficiently. There are so many displays and switches to learn. After a four-day absence from the cockpit, some sequences that should be automatic aren't. I'll still know where the adversary is and how I can lock him up, but my fingers may not do what I want them to do.

Putting fighter and attack missions together in the F/A-18 is a first for the Navy. An attack pilot has been taught from the beginning to organize, schedule, and work out every detail. A fighter pilot never has had to plan. He doesn't know about the mission, but he knows how to find MiGs, and he knows how to dogfight. The F/A-18 pilot has to make precise plans, but at the same time be flexible and innovative. A person unwilling to bend cannot perform both missions.

The men in this unit are self-starters. If they did well in the Navy, they're probably doing well in civilian life, and they'll continue to do well in the Naval Reserve. The commitment is no big deal; they just do their jobs.

—F/A-18 pilot
Naval Reserve, NAS Lemoore

Naval Reserve F/A-18s

Facing Air Force Reserve F-16s shadowing an active-duty Marine Corps F/A-18; **above** Naval Reserve F/A-18.

Montana
72476
Big Sky Country
03
S. AIR FORCE
120 th Ftr Intcp Grp Great Falls
72463
Big Sky Country
07

Pages 32-33 and right Montana Air National Guard F-106 Delta Darts.

I 'VE BEEN FLYING the F-106 for 15 years. There aren't many of them around anymore; if you talk to a supply guy who is trying to get parts for it, I guess the F-106 seems like an antique. I don't think pilots have noticed a big difference in performance over the years though, because the planes are so well maintained.

The F-106 is amazing for a 1959 airplane. Even then it was an all-weather, day or night interceptor, and now with modifications to the armament and fire control system, it's still in good shape. Features such as the TSD [tactical situation display] keep it fairly advanced.

Sure, it's not an F-15 or an F-16; the turn rate of the F-106 is limited compared with modern tactical fighters. Because the most difficult thing for me is to keep my eyes focused on a target right in front of me, I want to get into a turning fight, but the F-106 doesn't have inside-the-turn capability.

The F-106 is positive and smooth, with long wings that enable it to cruise at high speeds over long distances. We'll probably lose endurance and some speed when the unit converts to F-16s. I will really miss the long-range radar shot.

—F-106 pilot
New Jersey Air National Guard

Montana Air National Guard F-106s maintained with endless waxing of glossy enamel; **pages 36-37** *Delta Darts in a four-G landing break over Great Falls, Montana.*

Montana Air National Guard F-106

Pages 40-41 Naval Reserve F-14 Tomcat; *above* "Yellow Shirt" positioning a Naval Reserve F-14 for catapult aboard USS Ranger; *facing* Naval Reserve F-14 over Arizona combat range.

AIR COMBAT IS THE ANTITHESIS of commercial transport. The commercial airline business, the source of 90 percent of reserve pilots, moves people as smoothly as possible from point A to point B. There's nothing smooth and calm about fighters. It's a violent world, charged with competition, whether it's within a squadron, between squadrons, or between reserves and regulars. If you don't like to compete, you're in the wrong business.

Taking off in an airplane that can go Mach 2 and then coming home to have dinner with your wife that night instead of being stuck aboard ship in the middle of the ocean—you'd be a fool not to like it.

—F-14 pilot

Naval Reserve, NAS Miramar

MOST PEOPLE THINK we're "weekend warriors," but nothing could be further from the truth. Each year we participate in 48 regular drills and 72 special ones; we're on active duty 14 days. We've had fliers out for as many as 120 days of active duty in addition to their drills — all that and full-time civilian careers, too.

Every member of a squadron has been hand-picked for the unit. Esprit de corps here is very real, particularly among senior enlisted men. After a missile shoot, aircrews don't just come back expecting pats on the back. Our maintenance personnel do an excellent job. The men who give us good engines take just as much pride in winning competitions as we do.

There's a lot of personal sacrifice. Almost everyone has a family. You miss ballet recitals, soccer games, your anniversary. It takes a very special family to balance priorities between home, civilian job, and the reserves. All three things have to work well, or one of them will fail.

    —F-14 pilot

    Naval Reserve, NAS Dallas

Pages 44-45 Naval Reserve F-14 heading for the "trap" aboard USS Ranger; **facing** vapor trail of a Naval Reserve F-14 signals high positive G forces; **above** Naval Reserve F-14.

WHEN WE CHALLENGE THE NAVY REGULARS in competitions, they look at us as if to say, "You guys are in the reserves; we'll show you how it's done." They have a lot of new people in their crew. They don't realize that our ordnancemen are petty officers who have served in the Navy.

With all our training, loading missiles and guns is a piece of cake. It takes the regulars about twice as long as us to load their weapons into the F-14. When we finish, usually in about ten minutes, our gunner walks over and asks them if they need any help.

Many reservists have more seniority and expertise than people in the regular Navy. Most of our pilots are Vietnam vets who have flown in combat. It's kind of fun having to prove ourselves all over again.

—*F-14 ordnanceman*
Naval Reserve, NAS Dallas

Facing *Loading radar-guided Sparrow and heat-seeking Sidewinder missiles for North Dakota Air National Guard F-4s;* **above** *Naval Reserve F-14 dropping a long-range Phoenix missile over a Pacific test range.*

Facing *Naval Reserve A-4 Skyhawk and active-duty Navy F-14;* **left** *Naval Reserve A-4.*

I'M A DC-9 COMMERCIAL PILOT. Once a month, I get back to my A-4, kick the tires, light the fire, and go. The A-4 is the perfect airplane for the reserves. A lot of planes have complicated systems that need constant maintenance and careful handling, but the A-4 is a straightforward needle-and-ball airplane that works well and lasts a long time. That's part of the fun of flying it.

When you get into the A-4, the cockpit rails hit you right on top of your shoulders. Once in the seat, you're really scrunched. Pull the canopy down, and it touches your head, so you kind of hunch over. Even so, it's a plane that feels good.

I cut my teeth on the A-4; I flew it in my advanced jet training, and it was the second airplane I had on a carrier. After logging 1,000 hours in the A-6, I was able to make an easy transition back to the A-4. A pilot doesn't forget how to fly it; it's the bicycle of jets.

The single-seat A-4, particularly the Echo, is a dream machine so sweet it almost flies itself. You just think where you want the stick to go, and that's where it goes. The only thing that will make me give this up is an order.

— *A-4 pilot*
Naval Reserve, NAS Oceana

IN WEAPONS COMPETITION, the A-7 is notorious for dropping one bull's eye after another. Once I got 11 bulls out of 12. It was almost too much, so I didn't even try the last one. I don't think I could get such good results with any other plane, even the F-16.

Bombing is a kind of geometric analysis in which computers solve the equations. If a pilot drops bombs manually, he can probably figure the geometry three times in one pass, but a computer does it 25 times per second.

The A-7 and the F-111 had the forerunners of today's accurate computerized bombing systems. The biggest advantage now is that you don't have to dive in a straight line to deliver a bomb. Bombers can't afford to be predictable. Now we can deliver a bomb while we're in a turn because the computer compensates for the maneuver. The computer's not perfect, so sometimes we have to figure how much it's off and make up for that by fooling it. That's the trick to this system.

I can drive in off to the side, go into a 70 or 80 degree banking turn, and release a 2,000-pounder in a lateral toss when the target is lined up. The bomb drops within 20 feet of the target, close enough to rip the treads off a tank.

You can defend yourself in the A-7 if you have to. We have long enough legs [enough fuel] to keep moving until the enemy runs out of gas. Trying to stay down until the enemy has to go home, sometimes we end up getting jammed into the dirt and weeds.

A lot of single-seat fighter pilots don't like two-seat airplanes, but in a two-seater, I've got two heads and four eyes. Having flown with some excellent back-seaters in F-89s and F-4s, I've often said that a two-seat airplane with the same capabilities as a single-seater will bury a macho fighter pilot. A lot of people don't like to hear that.

The secret to flying fighters isn't in your hands, it's in your mind. That's one of the most difficult things for a student coming out of pilot training to realize. The best fighter pilots are the ones always thinking ahead of the airplane, calculating what might happen next and what the alternatives might be. We assume everyone can fly the airplane; what we want are people who can think. That's what makes the difference.

—*A-7 pilot*
Arizona Air National Guard

Pages 52-53 Four A-7K Corsairs of the Arizona Air National Guard; facing boom operator's view of an A-7K refueling.

I REALLY LIKE SINGLE-SEAT FLYING. It's like having a big toy box to yourself. You are the weapons system manager, radio operator, navigator, everything. Once you get used to handling all that, you don't want to give any of it up. Bombs fall on target or they don't, and there is no one else to blame.

When they started integrating all the systems in the A-7, they figured it took 1.3 people to fly it; when you add night capabilities like FLIR [forward-looking infrared], it jumps up to about 1.8. You have to manage all the systems effectively, fly the airplane, and keep it tactically oriented.

Then there's landing aboard ship, when any airplane is a challenge. The A-7 is known as one of the more difficult planes to land on a carrier because its faster approach speed and high critical wing make it want to glide. If you're coming in a little too fast and you bring the power back, you'll sail over the wires a lot faster than in other planes. Pull the power back too much, and the engine goes to sleep on you.

Recently, for the first time in ten years, my reserve unit did night landings. I was surprised and impressed. I had only been out of the Navy for six months, so I expected a circus. In active service, when we worked with new guys just out of a Replacement Air Group, it could be kind of colorful. But it was easy for us as reservists.

Our collective knowledge is greater than that of the fleet. Here, we don't get a new guy who walks in and says, "What's an airplane?" Most of us have a minimum of nine to ten years' flying experience with the Navy.

—A-7 pilot
Naval Reserve, NAS Alameda

Naval Reserve A-7

THE COCKPIT OF THE F-16 is well designed. You don't have to look down or touch anything on the instrument panel. Pilots hit one or more of five buttons under the fingers of each hand on both throttle and stick to control radio, radar, and weapons. We call it playing the piccolo.

For weapons deployment in the A-7, you have to select one station, prepare it, arm it, then hit the pickle button on the stick. In the F-16, there's one three-position arming switch. Air-to-ground weapons have a rotary dial for the bomb load.

The F-16 is programmed on the ground. Once airborne, you only work on the computer for a few things: to change destination, check winds, assess fuel. Sometimes a pilot can get confused by all the technology in an F-16; flight school bombards us with so much information it's like trying to drink water from a fire hose.

Flying fighters is more physically demanding these days. I used to fly three missions in the A-7, come back, order a sandwich and a Coke, and I'd be ready to go out again. In the F-16, you can get into a turning engagement and pull seven Gs for a while, even nine for short periods. It's draining. You have to prepare yourself mentally and physically before you pull the stick.

    —*F-16 pilot*
      South Carolina Air National Guard

*Pages 58-59 Air Force Reserve F-16 Fighting Falcon; **facing** Montana Air National Guard F-106 pilot training for transition to the F-16; **top left** F-16 throttle with weapons, radar, and radio controls; **top right** F-16 control stick; **below** an active-duty F-15 videotaped in the sights of a Texas Air National Guard F-16.*

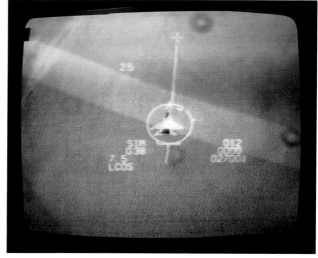

Pages 62-63 Air Force Reserve F-16s; **above** Arizona
Air National Guard F-16B.

Pages 66-67 *Active-duty A-10 Thunderbolts flown by Air Force Reserve pilots from bases in England and Germany;* **above** *self-portrait of Air Force Reserve Capt. "Uncle" Earl Deroche in an A-10 cockpit.*

THE A-10's LACK OF SPEED doesn't bother me, because at slower speeds I can see the target and watch it get hit. That makes us more vulnerable, but the A-10 was designed with a certain amount of survivability. To maintain contact with the target in close air support, we must be able to maneuver the airplane; I think that's why the A-10 has such straight, ugly wings. Flying low, we use the terrain, get behind rocks and close to trees. It's a challenging environment.

    —A-10 pilot
    Maryland Air National Guard

A-10 pilot navigating with road maps as well as aviation charts

Air Force Reserve A-10 dropping Mark 82 bombs;
facing A-10's seven-barrel 30 mm anti-tank gun
delivering as many as 65 rounds per second.

WHEN YOU SQUEEZE THE TRIGGER in an A-10, you get instant feedback. In three seconds you see what you have to do in subsequent attacks. It was difficult to get good scores in the F-4, but the first time I squeezed the trigger in the A-10, I scored 90 percent. The system has such accuracy and velocity that I can almost correct the second half of a burst. You sure feel the vibration; the gun's recoil is 17,000 pounds—the equivalent of a J79 afterburner. If you hold the trigger down long enough, you'll be thrust forward in the straps. Extreme vibration makes the G meter peg. When the needle jumps from plus 12 to minus 12 in the middle of a burst, it's absolutely useless.

    —A-10 pilot
    Maryland Air National Guard

WHEN THE PRESIDENT GIVES A DIRECTIVE to mobilize the Guard, we'll get the recall roster, phone everyone, and tell them to show up. They might call National Guard units on radio and television, too. Everyone will have his things packed and ready either at home or with the unit, depending on how each group's decided to work that. We've got 24 hours to get all our people back in their units and put them on active duty.

We'll have another day to get everyone up to speed. Sometimes we'll actually be running. Everyone will go through a process which includes paperwork and shots. Then we'll have briefings on our missions and find out how we'll be transported to them. While some people go through a line for paperwork, others will assemble cargo, weigh it, package it, and put it on pallets. Then we'll be ready to go.

The rules for our inspections are exactly the same as for the active duty. The deadlines are just the same, too, except the 24 extra hours we have to call our people in. Many of the airline pilots in my unit live as far away as Florida, Texas, and Chicago, so that time comes in handy.

—*F-4 squadron commander*
Michigan Air National Guard

Pages 72-73 *Marine Corps Reserve F-4 Phantom at MCAS Kaneohe, Hawaii;* ***facing and above*** *Alabama Air National Guard photo reconnaissance variants of the F-4.*

Facing *Hawaii Air National Guard F-4s in "missing man" formation over the USS Arizona Memorial, December 7, 1986;* **above** *Col. Tai "Mynah" Hong of the Hawaii Air National Guard, F-4 pilot for almost 25 years;* **pages 78-79** *Marine Corps Reserve F-4s over the coast of Molokai, Hawaii.*

SOMEONE ONCE DESCRIBED THE F-4 as a single-shot muzzle loader compared to the new fighters, which are more like machine guns in their delivery. In the F-4, we fly with blinders on, seeing only what's straight ahead. While we lock up and track one target at a time, new fighters can track multiple targets. Within the limits of visual range, though, we hold our own.

In the F-4, we have to fight a different fight. Against F-15s with conformal external fuel tanks, for instance, we really need to be waiting for them. When they come to our altitude with full tanks, their performance isn't much better than ours, especially if we've already burned a lot of fuel and weigh less.

Newer planes have better pitch and acceleration to turn on us, so we try to stay at a medium altitude, since that's where we make our best turns. We wait for them to make a mistake, and then we capitalize on that. If we can get them into a position where they have no advantage, then it becomes a matter of experience.

—F-4 radar intercept officer
Marine Corps Reserve, Andrews AFB

Left Fin flash on an Oregon Air National Guard F-4; **above** Hawaii Air National Guard F-4 taking off from Honolulu International Airport.

Pages 82-83 and above *Louisiana Air National Guard F-15 Eagles*

TODAY, MOST PRACTICE BATTLES are fought without pilots' ever seeing each other. The longer the reach of your radar, the sooner you can assess a situation and either decide to engage the enemy or evade before you're inside his weapons' range. The F-15 has the most powerful radar of any fighter built.

The F-15 also has a perfect complement of ordnance: a 20 mm gun that strikes from 3,000 feet until you ram; AIM-9 heat-seeking missiles that, allowing for closing speeds, have a range of five miles if you're in front of the enemy's nose. The AIM-7 radar missile reaches much farther than that, even through the clouds. We can fire missiles at two enemy planes at the same time.

It takes a lot of energy to turn an airplane, and the thrust of an F-15 allows it to sustain a turning fight when other fighters would be falling out of the sky. The twist in the F-15's cambered wings makes it possible to increase angle of attack at slow speeds without stalling. The price paid for this maneuverability is drag; it's supposed to be a Mach 2.5 airplane, but I've never flown it at more than 2.1. Even then it's just to get in and get out in a hurry.

　　—F-15 pilot
　　Louisiana Air National Guard

*Louisiana Air National Guard F-15 Eagle; **pages 86-87** Louisiana Air National Guard Lt. Col. Jack "Flounder" Boh zeroing in on an active-duty F-16; **pages 88-89** Louisiana Air National Guard F-15s in delta formation; **pages 90-91** Louisiana Air National Guard F-15.*

AIRLIFT/TANKER

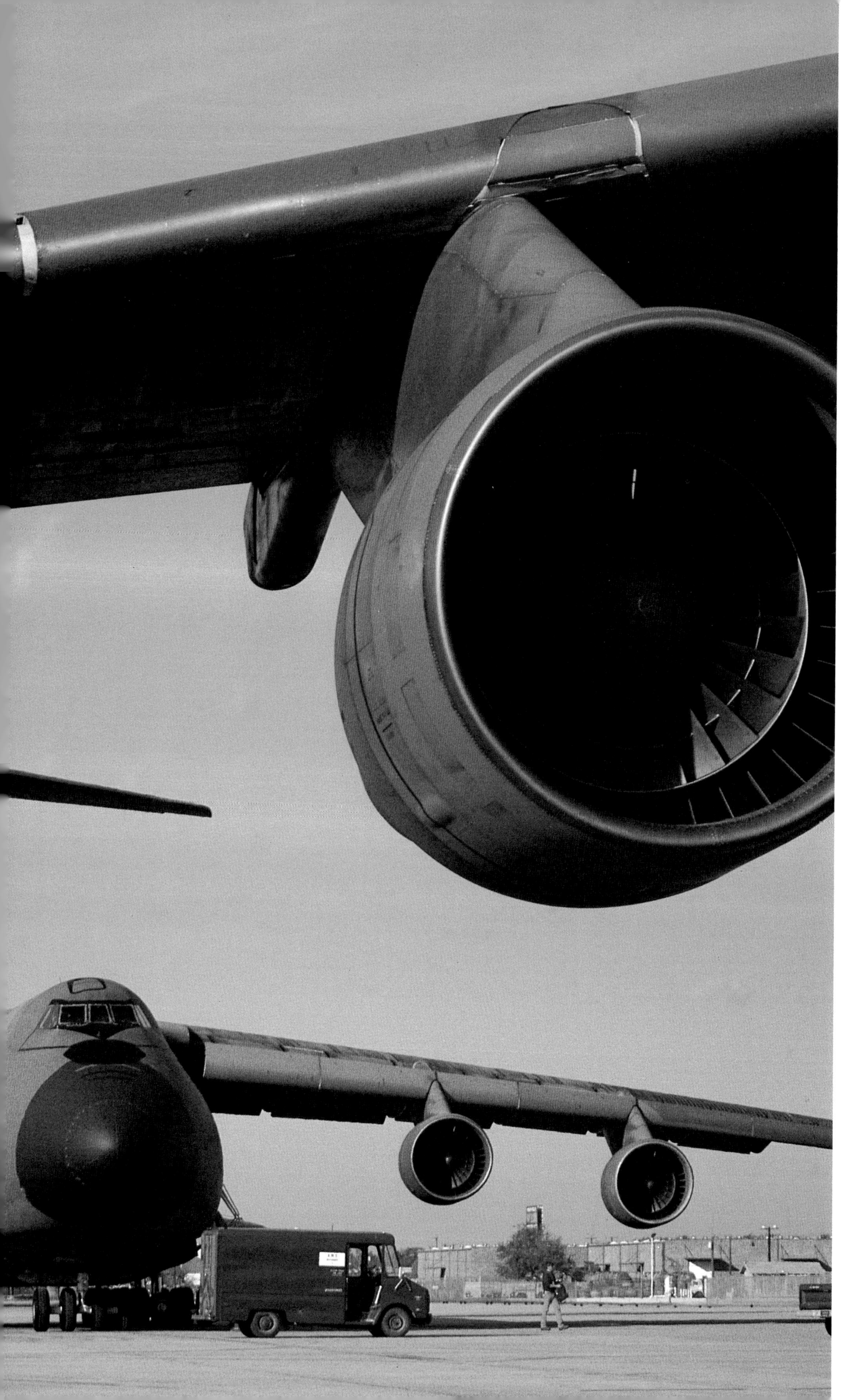

PERATING THE BOOM SMOOTHLY is like greasing a landing. It's a matter of pride to lay the refueling nozzle into the receiver instead of slamming it, to have some softness in the contact.

In the KC-10, the boom control stick moves left to right like the stick in an F-16. You can fly the boom with two fingers. The system fatigue on the KC-10 is probably one-third to one-half that of the KC-135. I've flown an eight-hour mission in the KC-10, controlling the boom from a chair, and had such a good time that it seemed to last only 15 or 20 minutes. In the KC-135, where the boom operator has to lie down to deliver the fuel, a four-hour mission wears you out, especially your neck.

In-flight refueling is inherently dangerous. It amazes me that it hasn't brought more aircraft out of the sky. We have a paragraph in our operation manual about airplanes flying in close proximity that will raise the hair on your back.

We've seen interesting situations on both ends of the boom. Last month, for the first time, I had an F-4 on the boom in bad weather. He was 32 feet away from me when I lost visual contact. For 15 seconds I couldn't see him. In normal weather with experienced people, refueling is all right, but at night, in adverse weather, it's downright scary.

—*KC-10 boom operator*
Air Force Reserve, March AFB

Pages 92-93 *Air Force Reserve C-5 Galaxies;* **pages 94-95** *Air Force Reserve KC-10 Extender;* **above** *Air National Guard F-4 approaching refueling boom of an Air Force Reserve KC-10;* **facing** *view from the rear seat of a Louisiana Air National Guard F-15 refueling from an Air Force Reserve KC-10;* **pages 98-99** *Oregon Air National Guard F-4s and an Air Force Reserve KC-10.*

THE C-141 IS NOT VERY MANEUVERABLE, so you really have to anticipate what the airplane is going to do. One morning after I'd made my transition from the T-38 to the C-141, the Air Force hauled me out of bed to find out whether I could land a big plane in a 25-knot crosswind. They didn't make the other students do this, but they were going to put me up there. When I asked why, they said they wanted to find out whether a woman could handle it. My instructor talked me through the landing, and after I put the C-141 on the ground, I went back to sleep, and that was that.

I moved into the Air Force Reserve pilot training program after graduating from ROTC, so I've never served in the active Air Force. I came into this squadron as the first USAF Reserve woman pilot and the first woman C-141 pilot. The guys in this unit had open minds—they waited to see what I could do before they made judgments—so it's worked out fine.

Women aren't allowed to make air drops because those are combat maneuvers, but we can refuel. I'm qualified as a copilot for this, and when I can, I'll probably go back to school for the additional training necessary to be a command pilot during refueling.

My husband's a C-141 pilot on active duty. The main difference between active duty and the reserves is that the reserves give you more control over your life. My husband and I have agreed that it is impossible to have two active-duty flying careers and still raise a family. We have the best of both worlds.

    —C-141 pilot
      Air Force Reserve, McGuire AFB

*Active-duty C-141 Starlifter flown by an Air Force
Reserve crew*

ABOARD SHIP THEY SAY, "Landing a Whale, clear the deck." Everyone has that feeling when the A-3 lands. I learned to fly it after the S-2 and A-4, so I was very impressed with its size. With experience, I've become more comfortable with the A-3. The most difficult part of a pilot's transition to the A-3 is landing. Things can be going great, with everything set up, then within 50 feet of the ground, it gets a mind of its own and seems to take over. In the A-3, no two landings are alike.

When you're in trouble in the A-3, there is always something you can do; there's a back door for everything. Still, a lot of pilots are apprehensive about flying without ejection seats. The Air Force version had them, but adding them would have made the Navy version too heavy for the carrier. That's where the old saying "All Three Dead" [from the old designation A3D] came from. Since many of us have flown with ejection seats, we still have nagging thoughts, especially when we roll down the catapult.

— *A-3 pilot*
Naval Reserve, NAS Alameda

Pages 102-103 *Naval Reserve KA-3 Skywarrior refueling an F-14;* ***above*** *Naval Reserve KA-3 aboard USS Ranger.*

Pages 106-107 *Air Force Reserve C-5 Galaxy;* **above** *Galaxy crew chief signaling engine start.*

Flight deck of a C-5

WE NEVER FEEL CRAMPED on the flight deck of the C-5. We can walk all over the place, even sit down at a table in the galley instead of eating off plates in our laps. The C-5 has a relaxation area and bunks for the crew. The roominess has a good psychological effect on us.

Coming to the C-5 with six years' experience as a fighter pilot, I was amazed at the airplane's responsiveness. Its handling capabilities are phenomenal. Once you get the C-5 in the air, you lose sight of the fact that you've got a massive airplane behind you. It's as if you're just flying the cockpit around.

Maneuvering on the ground is a different proposition. With a wingspan of 220 feet and a length of 250 feet, the C-5 is a nightmare to taxi, unless it's going into a field specifically set up for jumbo aircraft. We fly into some places that weren't measured very well before they were classified big enough for C-5s. If we're not careful, we'll get ourselves into a box.

A pilot turns a 727 or DC-9 by this rule of thumb: if you can clear the nose of the airplane, you can clear the wing. Those guys taxi around as if they were driving cars. You can't do that with a C-5. You have a certain feel for it, but when you get within 25 feet, you can't trust your eyes anymore. You have to let someone else guide you.

 —*C-5 pilot*

  Air Force Reserve, Dover AFB

Left Air Force Reserve C-5; **above** maintenance officer Lt. John Silvia inside the C-5's vertical stabilizer.

*Washington KC-135 refueling a North Dakota F-4 while Montana
F-106s wait their turns in a gathering of Air National Guard planes.*

Pages 114-115 California Air National Guard search and rescue HC-130 Hercules; *above* new C-130 ready for delivery; *facing* California Air National Guard C-130.

I T ALWAYS SURPRISES ME when an Air Force guy says, "Oh, you're in the Guard—that's the best kept secret around." In a sense, we're in our own world. We fly with the regular Air Force, but when we land, our aircrewmen will stay together if they can.

The relaxed atmosphere in the reserves is great. I'm not good at being rank conscious; I don't care if someone's a general or a lieutenant if he is okay otherwise. There's friendship in a crew where everyone knows everyone else's strengths and weaknesses. Crew members watch out for each other. If I had to choose between going to war with the Air Force and going to war with this unit, I'd go with this unit.

—C-130 pilot
West Virginia Air National Guard

*California Air National Guard HC-130 refueling
HH-3 Jolly Green Giants*

WHEN A P-3 CREW IS ASSIGNED ASW [antisubmarine warfare], we deploy buoys that operate like radio stations. Passive buoys listen to sounds made in the water, while active buoys work like sonar to send out sounds that bounce off things. The echo gives us direction and distance information. We usually stay out for 12 to 14 hours; whether we detect anything depends on how good the intelligence is for the area we patrol.

The variety of my crew is typical for a P-3. I'm a 727 captain for Continental Airlines, my copilot is a flight instructor for the Singer Corporation finishing his masters in computer science, and the third copilot has a job with a defense contractor. One flight engineer also works in P-3s for U.S. Customs, and the second is full-time active duty. Our radioman works for the Chamber of Commerce in New Orleans. The center console operator is an undergraduate in electrical engineering. The navigator is an executive at Exxon. The tactical coordinator is a computer programmer for NASA. Sensor one sells avionics, and sensor two is full-time active duty. The ordnanceman runs a contracting company.

    —P-3 pilot
    Naval Reserve, NAS New Orleans

Pages 120-121 Air Force Reserve WC-130 Hercules prepared to take off for a hurricane watch; pages 122-123 Naval Reserve P-3 Orion, its two outboard engines cold and feathered, on submarine patrol over the Pacific; facing Naval Reserve P-3; above Lt. Cdr. Bo Norton and Lt. Cdr. Chris Cluster in a Naval Reserve P-3 cockpit.

Naval Reserve E-2 Hawkeye being catapulted from USS Ranger; **facing** *Cdr. J.J. Johannsen at one of three scope positions in a Naval Reserve E-2.*

THE PRIMARY MISSION OF THE E-2 is airborne early warning, identification, and engagement of hostile aircraft threatening the battle group. We give tactical support, make bogey calls, and monitor electronic signals around a battle group. We also provide search and rescue assistance.

We are often asked to do all of this at the same time. With only three controllers and five radios in the back, we have to be masters at juggling. Sometimes people get frustrated with us because they don't understand that a controller can't stop everything he's doing to help them. It takes a long time to get a good working relationship with the ship and the airwing.

Our radar can cover millions of square miles. We can vector aircraft toward surface ships for identification and determine whether they're making any hostile moves. If Russian intelligence-gathering aircraft appear, an air control officer and a radar officer work on the solution to intercept.

When you're identifying Soviet aircraft, your adrenalin pops up. The lives of 5,000 men in the battle group depend on how well you do your job.

—*E-2 controller*
Naval Reserve, NAS Miramar

HELICOPTERS

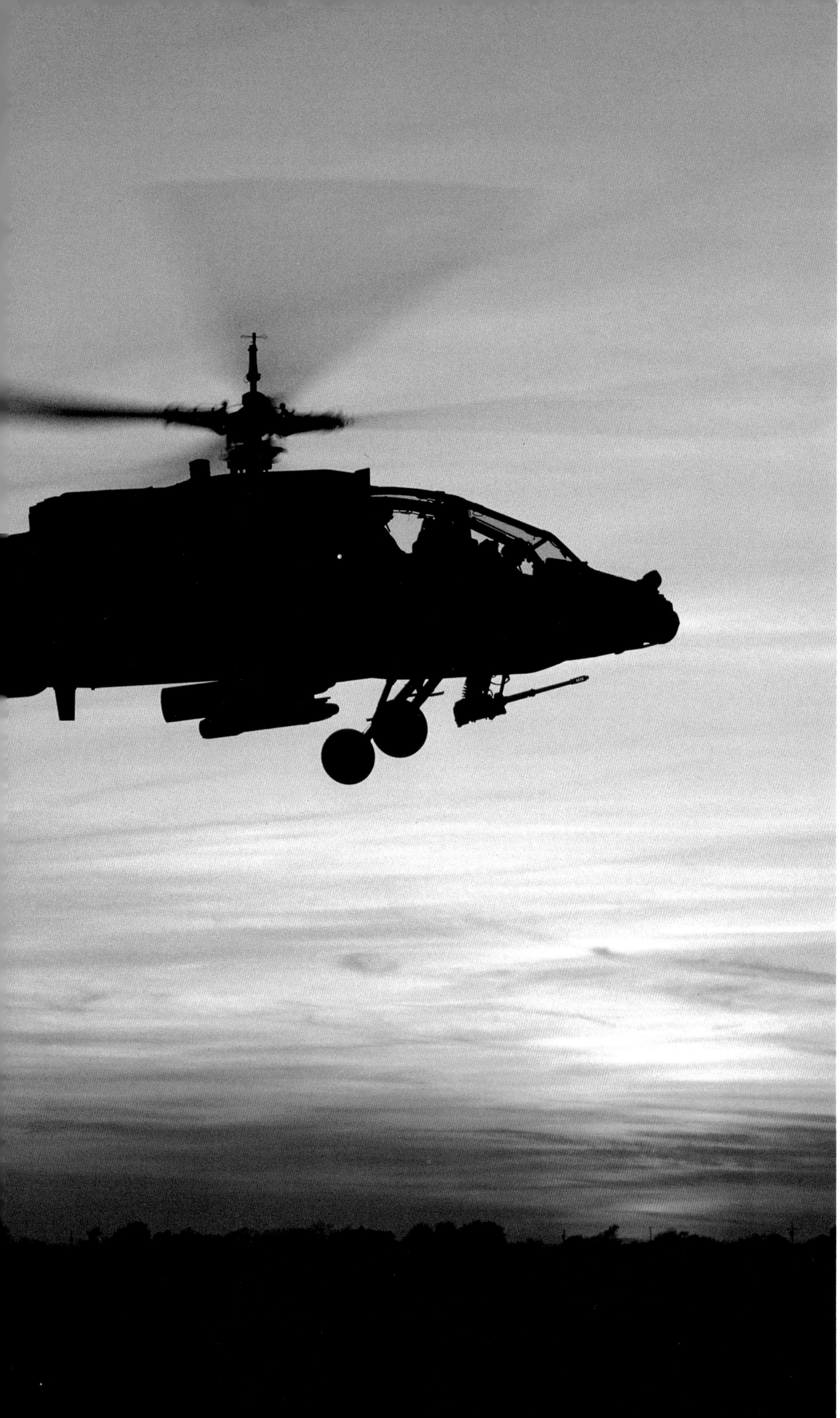

THE HUEY WAS DESIGNED for medical evacuation; it's a simple aircraft with a single, reliable hydraulic system and a turbine engine that can take bullet holes and still bring you home. Although the Huey was designed for a single mission, we also made it into a successful utility and gunship.

It will be a while before the UH-60 utility helicopter can replace the UH-1. Unlike the Hueys, the UH-60s don't have particle separators to protect their new engines from sand. After 200 hours' flying time over deserts in Egypt, the UH-60's engines had to be replaced because of abrasion. Hueys can survive that.

The airframe and skids of the Huey are so strong you can slam the machine into the ground without really hurting it. Any pilot has bent some skids if he's flown long enough. Anyone who has gone in and out of tight landing zones has had to cut a way in and out. Huey rotors are tough enough for that; they'll chop through small twigs and branches without much damage. Once I crashed a Huey into a teak tree from a 200-foot hover. I'm still here because the helicopter could take it.

In Vietnam, Hueys returned from combat missing parts they were never designed to fly without. The Huey was the B-17 of the Vietnam War.

—UH-1 pilot
Army Reserve, Ft. Meade

Pages 128-129 *North Carolina Army National Guard AH-64 Apache;* **facing** *parachute drop from Marine Corps Reserve UH-1 Iroquois;* **above** *Army Reserve UH-1.*

California Air National Guard HH-3s

Above and facing New York Air National Guard
HH-3s.

SEARCH AND RESCUE are the HH-3's prime missions. Even the Coast Guard doesn't make rescues beyond 200 miles from shore. At night, when you're hovering over a ship that's pitching and breaking up in 40-foot seas, it's difficult to keep from getting tangled up in the rigging. Sometimes the people on the boat are safer than we are.

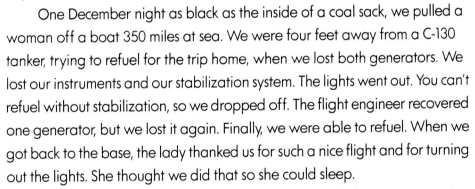

I don't think most rescued people realize that they're strapped to 20,000 pounds of flailing metal just as dangerous as the boat that's sinking. If we're hovering over a ship and one of our engines coughs, we'll be part of the ship fast.

One December night as black as the inside of a coal sack, we pulled a woman off a boat 350 miles at sea. We were four feet away from a C-130 tanker, trying to refuel for the trip home, when we lost both generators. We lost our instruments and our stabilization system. The lights went out. You can't refuel without stabilization, so we dropped off. The flight engineer recovered one generator, but we lost it again. Finally, we were able to refuel. When we got back to the base, the lady thanked us for such a nice flight and for turning out the lights. She thought we did that so she could sleep.

In search and rescue, you often go beyond your fuel range. You can't carry all the fuel you need, because when you hover and rescue off a ship, you can't afford the weight. You have to jettison some and count on C-130s for refueling.

When I first started refueling, it was hell, particularly at night and in turbulence. It's more dangerous with helicopters than it is with fixed-wing aircraft. When we refuel in the HH-3, our rotor blade tips are just 15 feet from the C-130's horizontal stabilizer. There's no room for error.

We do all this in a 1957 vintage helicopter. I wouldn't drive the same distance in a 1957 car. Reporters on shore wonder what's the big deal—they fly over the ocean all the time in airliners. After we've been aloft for almost 14 hours, refueling four times at 200 feet in the rain, they ask, "Did anything exciting happen?"

—HH-3 pilot
New York Air National Guard

Pages 136-137, above, and facing
California Army National Guard CH-47
Chinooks.

I ENJOY THE CH-47 because it's so different from the Boeing 737 I fly commercially. In a 737, you jump in, climb, switch on the autopilot, and drum your fingers; in a CH-47, you fly low, see things, and don't have to rush.

The difference between the Chinook and other helicopters is like the difference between a Cadillac and a sports car. If you clown around with the Chinook, it won't respond well. Treat it deliberately, and it will do all the work for you.

The CH-47 carries a gun crew and ammo inside and artillery outside. We can recover men and their rafts while we're floating on a river. We're always on standby for hurricanes and floods, any disasters that require us to be in the water.

—CH-47 pilot
Pennsylvania Army National Guard

WHEN I WAS AN ATTACK PILOT in Vietnam, the old gunships were sufficient. The modernization of armies on both sides has demanded something different. The Apache is the best answer I've seen. It's so much more advanced than helicopters I flew before that I was at a loss when I first crawled into it.

There are three ways to detect targets in the AH-64. You can find them directly through a telescope, through a kind of TV camera that uses enough infrared to locate tanks at dusk, or with FLIR [forward-looking infrared] that works passively, without a radar or laser beam that might give you away. At night, FLIR enables us to see tank tracks that hold residual heat from the sun.

A helmet-mounted bore sight in front of my right eye directs the fire control computer electronically to wherever my head is pointed. I put the cross hairs on the target, then fire the laser, which gives the range. The fire control computer registers the distance to the tank in meters, say 4,236. At that distance, I'm not going to hit it, particularly if it's a heavy tank, unless I use a Hellfire missile.

Once fired, the missile comes off the rail, pitches up 19 degrees, and climbs to about 2,600 feet. When it starts coming down on a programmed trajectory, I hit the target with my laser. The missile picks up the energy using an infrared seeker in its head, makes the final adjustment when I lase for terminal guidance, then hits the target. The steepest angles make the best kills.

—*AH-64 pilot*
North Carolina Army National Guard

Facing *AH-64 instrument panel displaying
night-viewing equipment;* **above** *North Carolina
Army National Guard AH-64*

THE UH-60 ISN'T COMPLETELY AUTOMATIC, but it's capable of hands-off flight. When it's hovering, you can put your feet flat on the floor, take your hands off the cyclic [stick], pull all the collective [main rotor control] you want, and the Black Hawk will go straight up. You might get some drift because of wind, but otherwise you'll keep a perfect heading. That takes a lot of getting used to.

The Black Hawk carries twice as much external cargo as the Huey, but seat for seat it carries about the same interior load. When we're simulating combat, everyone has to wear seat belts, but in real combat we'll probably just pull the seats out, pack 20 men in, put a strap across the side doors, and go for it.

In the Black Hawk, you might run out of space, but not out of power; we have more than we ever need. We can even pull a few negative Gs. In the Huey, there's a lag between moving the cyclic right and the helicopter's moving right. Not in the Black Hawk.

The UH-60 has greater capabilities than the UH-1, but its complexity makes it more difficult to repair in the field. Black Hawk pilots tease Huey pilots, saying, "Skids are for kids," but they come right back to us and say, "When the last Black Hawk goes to the boneyard, the Huey will fly the crew out."

— *UH-60 pilot*
Virginia Army National Guard

Facing and above Army light infantrymen rappelling from a Virginia Army National Guard UH-60 Black Hawk.

THE COBRA'S MAIN MISSION is armed escort and destruction of enemy
tanks. The back-seater in the AH-1 is usually the pilot in command,
since he has all the radios and a lot of the instruments. He also shoots the
rockets. The pilot in the front seat usually navigates and fires the gun, aiming
with the turret controls that make the gun traverse. When you're in the front
seat, you're on a magic carpet ride, out in the middle of nothing, zipping
over the ground.

There's no automatic flight control system—it's strictly seat-of-the-pants
flying. Let go of the stick, and you'll dive to the left. The Cobra will try
to kill you. Even though I've been in an AH-1 squadron for 12 years, I still
learn something new every time I fly.

I have a theory that when we go to war, the reserves will have an
advantage over everyone else, because when things break down, we'll
know how to fix them. The AH-1 is simple and it keeps going, as long as
you have a few parts and good maintenance. In wartime, the Cobras will
be down there sneaking around, providing fire support for the guys on the
ground.

Ordnance crews are made up of tough guys who can handle working
24-hour days without complaint. Sometimes when we're tired, we see those
guys working so hard—it motivates the rest of us. I wish they could ride in
the front seat of the Cobra and shoot the gun just once.

    —AH-1 pilot
    Marine Corps Reserve, NAS Atlanta

Utah Army National Guard OH-6 Cayuse

WE FLY IN AND OUT OF DANGEROUS AREAS in the OH-6, hunting for enemy tanks and soldiers, then we lead the gun guys in the AH-1 to the target.

I thought the OH-6 was great the first time I flew it, and after more than 3,000 hours of flight, I still do. It's small and responsive. Everything is mechanically linked, so you really fly the helicopter, not the system. Flying low in the OH-6, you can experience the ground without quite touching down with your feet.

The biggest problem with the OH-6 is getting parts. We have to get many of them commercially now, and it's expensive. I guess the only future for the OH-6 is crop dusting or display in a museum.

—OH-6 pilot
Maryland Army National Guard

Left Checking a rotor of a Marine Corps Reserve CH-53 Sea Stallion; **below** *New York Air National Guard maintenance of an HH-3 Jolly Green Giant;* **pages 150-151** *Marine Corps Reserve CH-53.*

SEEN FROM THE COCKPIT down the back, the CH-53 looks like a Greyhound bus built to transfer a gun crew, howitzers, ammunition, and a jeep. The Marine Corps relies on the CH-46 to carry troops, but when the Corps is in a bind, we can transport troops, too.

The CH-53's articulated rotary wing enables its six blades to tilt vertically, slant horizontally, and rotate. All of this contributes to the helicopter's smooth ride, though watching a slow-motion film of the way the blades move in flight would probably make a lot of people reluctant to get in a helicopter again.

We have so many roles to perform in the CH-53 that flying it never really gets boring. We work with the guys on the ground a lot, so we understand what they need. We can carry water buffaloes and howitzers in our cargo net, transport troops to the front line for low-level combat assault, drop paratroops out the back, fly at night, and land on ships and even mountains.

—*CH-53 pilot*
Marine Corps Reserve, NAS Dallas

Arizona Air National Guard F-16

THE PHOTOGRAPHS IN THIS BOOK were taken with a battered collection of Nikon 35 mm cameras, primarily motor-driven F-3s and N-2000s, plus a score of lenses ranging from 16 mm fisheyes to 500 mm telephotos. The cameras were unmodified and no filters were used. Almost all the photographs were taken with Kodachrome 64 slide film.

A number of head-on and tail-chase images were taken by cameras mounted in a remote-controlled pod suspended from an underwing weapons station. My thanks to all the superb Reserve and Guard pilots who did the driving for me.

—*George Hall*

AIRCRAFT FACTS

F/A-18 HORNET

The F/A-18 is a multi-mission, high-performance tactical aircraft that executes fighter, strike, and intercept missions from both aircraft carriers and shore bases.

The design of the F/A-18 incorporates carbon/epoxy composite materials known for their strength, light weight, and resistance to corrosion. Fewer parts and greater accessibility to each of them ensure easier maintenance and better reliability.

The Hornet's dual-mode advanced radar, laser detector tracker (LDT), and forward-looking infrared sensor (FLIR) enable the aircraft to attack in all weather conditions and at night. A raid assessment mode allows identification of closely spaced targets by increasing radar resolution. The F/A-18's radar system can produce ground maps for identification and navigation.

Primary function: multi-mission fighter and attack aircraft
Prime contractor: McDonnell Aircraft Company, McDonnell Douglas Corporation
Power plant: two General Electric F404-GE-400 turbofan engines, 16,000 pounds thrust each
Dimensions: wingspan 37 feet 6 inches, length 56 feet, height 15 feet 3 inches
Speed: Mach 1.7
Ceiling: over 50,000 feet
Combat radius: fighter over 460 miles, attack over 630 miles
Armament: one 20 mm MK-61 Vulcan cannon, fighter—Sparrow and Sidewinder missiles; attack—guided and conventional air-to-ground ordnance
Maximum takeoff weight: fighter—35,000 pounds, attack—51,900 pounds
Crew: one—pilot

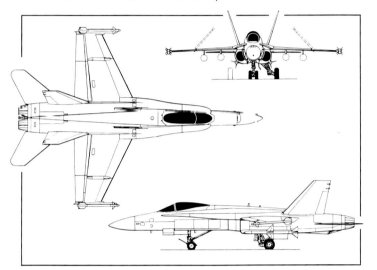

F-106 DELTA DART
NICKNAME: SIX

A supersonic, all weather interceptor, the F-106 was developed from the F-102 to accommodate the more powerful J75 turbojet engine and advanced electronic components. It was the primary manned interceptor aircraft in the U.S. Air Force throughout the 1960s and 1970s.

The F-106 is equipped with the Hughes MA-1 electronic guidance and fire control system, capable of seeking several targets at once. It works with the Joint Surveillance System/Region Operations Control Center (JSS/ROCC) computer-guided radar that can determine the location of aircraft within its range, calculate the best course of intercept, and relay the information back to the aircraft.

Primary function: interceptor
Prime contractor: Convair Division, General Dynamics Corporation
Power plant: one Pratt & Whitney J75-P-17 turbojet engine with 24,500 pounds thrust
Dimensions: wingspan 38 feet 1 inch, length 70 feet 7 inches, height 20 feet 3 inches
Speed: Mach 2
Ceiling: above 50,000 feet
Range: beyond 1,500 miles
Armament: four AIM-4F/G Falcon missiles, one AIR-2A Genie missile, 20 mm M-61 Vulcan multibarrel gun
Maximum takeoff weight: 43,000 pounds
Crew: one—pilot

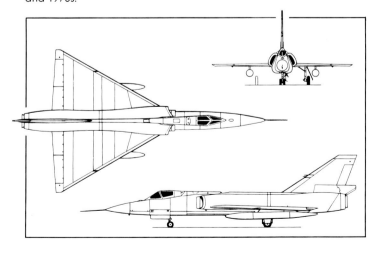

F-14 TOMCAT
NICKNAME: TURKEY

The F-14 is a twin-engine, variable-sweep wing, supersonic fighter. A computer automatically changes the wing sweep for optimum aerodynamic efficiency, even during high-G maneuvers. Other features contributing to the F-14's remarkable performance include a horizontal stabilizer that operates for roll as well as pitch control, twin rudders that give directional control even under the asymmetric load conditions of missile firing, and a sculpted fuselage that forms more than half the total aerodynamic lifting surface.

The F-14's AWG-9 weapons system can attack 6 different targets simultaneously while it tracks 18 others. The look-down/shoot-down radar, performing against both opening and closing targets, directs the launching of missiles and the firing of the M-61 cannon. It can discern fighter-size targets at more than 100 miles across a 120 mile-wide scan sector, with high resistance to electronic countermeasures. A two-way digital link allows the transfer of data to surface and airborne intercept. A camera in the F-14's nose has a 10:1-magnification TV sight that provides visual target identification at long range.

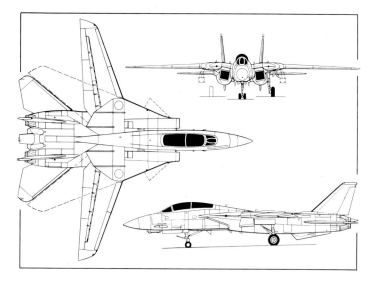

Primary function: intercept of multiple airborne targets in all weather conditions and at night
Prime contractor: Grumman Aerospace Corporation
Power plant: two Pratt & Whitney TF30-P-414A turbofan engines, 20,000 pounds thrust each
Dimensions: wingspan 64 feet 1 inch (fully extended), length 62 feet 9 inches, height 16 feet
Speed: Mach 2
Ceiling: above 50,000 feet
Combat radius: 578 miles
Armament: six Phoenix, four Sparrow, and four Sidewinder missiles; one 20 mm MK-61A1 Vulcan cannon
Maximum takeoff weight: 62,260 pounds
Crew: two—pilot, radar intercept officer

A-4 SKYHAWK
NICKNAME: SCOOTER

The A-4 Skyhawk is a lightweight attack and ground-support aircraft that was designed to replace the prop-driven A-1 Skyraider. The A-4 has a modified delta low-aspect-ratio wing with moderate wing loading.

The aircraft's configuration gives it excellent low-altitude, high-speed capabilities. Skyhawk ordnance includes two 20 mm cannon, rockets, missiles, and a variety of bombs which can be delivered by lay-down, glide, loft, and air- and ground-designated modes. Ordnance stores are carried externally on pylons and racks under the fuselage and wings. The Skyhawk can also deliver nuclear weapons.

Other roles of the A-4 are to serve as air controller, simulate "bogeys" in air combat training, and tow aerial targets. One configuration serves as an advanced jet trainer.

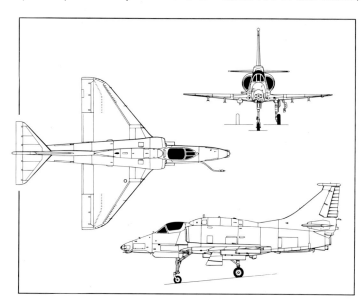

Primary function: light attack, air combat training, aerial tow
Prime contractor: Douglas Aircraft Company, McDonnell Douglas Corporation
Power plant: A-4E/F—J52-P-8A engine with 9,300 pounds thrust; A-4M—J52-P-408 engine with 11,200 pounds thrust
Dimensions: wingspan 27 feet 6 inches, length 41 feet 4 inches, height 15 feet
Speed: 685 mph
Ceiling: 40,450 feet
Range: 1,380 miles with external tanks
Armament: two 20 mm cannon, rockets, missiles, and bombs carried externally
Maximum takeoff weight: 24,500 pounds
Crew: one—pilot, or two—pilot and weapons system officer/observer

A-7 CORSAIR II
NICKNAME: SLUF (Short Little Ugly Fella)

The Corsair II is a light attack plane with a microminiaturized digital computer that increases weapons delivery accuracy. A head-up display (HUD) presents continuous cues for bombing and navigation directly in front of the pilot's eyes, enabling him to concentrate on his mission without reference to cockpit instruments. With the central digital computer calling signals and solutions, the pilot can execute level, dive, or toss bomb drops at ground targets with great precision.

The computer-directed map navigation system stores maps that cover a million square miles on a single roll of 35 mm film. Avionics features include Doppler and forward-looking radar and an inertial measuring unit.

Primary function: air support of front-line troops and tactical zone bombing
Primary contractor: Vought Aeronautics Division of LTV Aerospace Corporation
Power plant: A-7D—Allison TF41-1 engine with 14,250 pounds thrust; A-7E—Allison TF41-A-2 engine with 15,000 pounds thrust
Dimensions: wingspan 38 feet 9 inches, length 46 feet 1 inch, height 16 feet 1 inch
Speed: 690 mph
Range: ferry 2,857 miles (maximum internal and external fuel)
Armament: 15,000 pounds of bombs and rockets, Sidewinder missiles, one M-61 Vulcan cannon
Maximum takeoff weight: 42,000 pounds
Crew: A-7D/E—one—pilot; A-7K—two—pilot, student pilot

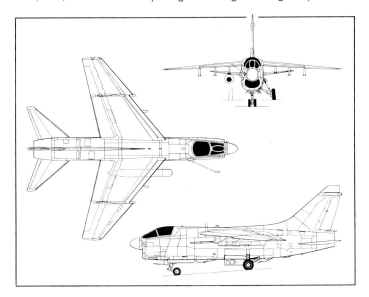

F-16 FIGHTING FALCON
NICKNAME: ELECTRIC JET

The F-16 Fighting Falcon is a highly maneuverable, compact, all-weather aircraft designed for air-to-air combat and air-to-surface attack.

The F-16 has excellent maneuverability; its small size and smokeless engine make it difficult to detect either visually or with radar. A 360-degree threat warning system reduces the possibility of the pilot being caught by surprise.

The aircraft's blended-body-and-wing design increases lift at high angles of attack and decreases drag. Leading and trailing edge flaps automatically change contour to give maximum lift-to-drag ratio and minimum buffet through all angles of flight.

The cockpit and its bubble canopy give the pilot almost unlimited visibility, and the fire control system—including radar, head-up display, and controls—eliminates any need for the pilot to look away from the target. Capable of tracking low-flying targets against ground clutter, it delivers weapons with superior accuracy.

Primary function: fighter, attack
Prime contractor: General Dynamics Corporation
Power plant: one Pratt & Whitney F100-PW-100 turbofan engine with 25,000 pounds thrust
Dimensions: wingspan 32 feet 8 inches, length 49 feet 5 inches, height 16 feet
Speed: Mach 2
Ceiling: above 50,000 feet
Range: ferry more than 2,000 miles
Armament: one M-61A1 20 mm multibarrel cannon, external stations with up to six AIM-9 Sidewinder missiles, conventional air-to-air and air-to-surface munitions, and electronic countermeasure pods
Maximum takeoff weight: 35,400 pounds
Crew: F-16A—one—pilot, F-16B—two—pilot, weapons operator or student pilot

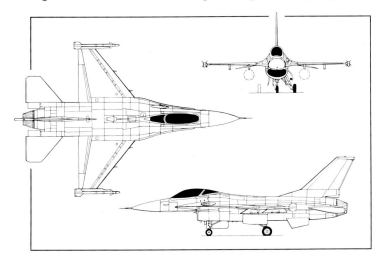

A-10 THUNDERBOLT II
NICKNAME: HOG, WARTHOG

The first Air Force aircraft designed specifically for close air support of ground forces, the A-10 Thunderbolt can be used effectively in adverse weather and poor visibility against all ground targets, including armored vehicles.

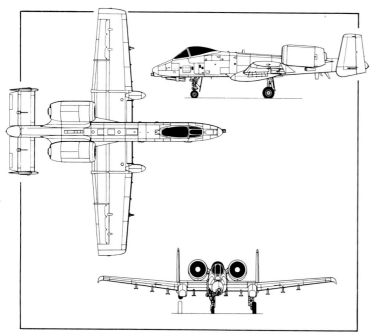

The A-10's short takeoff and landing capability permits operations near front lines. Many parts are interchangeable, and redundant structural components enable the A-10 to withstand heavy damage and survive direct hits from armor-piercing and high-explosive projectiles.

The weapons delivery system includes a head-up display and a laser target-seeking pod under the fuselage. The A-10 has infrared and electronic defense against surface-to-air missiles.

Primary function: close air support
Prime contractor: Fairchild Republic Company
Power plant: two General Electric TF34-GE-100 turbofan engines, 8,900 pounds thrust each
Dimensions: wingspan 57 feet 6 inches, length 53 feet 4 inches, height 14 feet 8 inches
Speed: 423 mph
Ceiling: can operate under 1,000 feet with one-mile visibility
Range: 250 miles with 9,500 pounds of ordnance and 1.8-hour loiter time
Armament: one GAU-8A 30 mm seven-barrel Gatling gun, up to 16,000 pounds mixed ordnance including 500-pound retarded bombs, 2,000-pound general purpose bombs, incendiary and Rockeye II cluster bombs, Maverick missiles, laser-guided/electro-optically guided bombs, infrared countermeasure flares, electronic countermeasure chaff, and jammer pods
Maximum takeoff weight: 46,038 pounds
Crew: one—pilot

F-4 PHANTOM II
NICKNAME: DOUBLE UGLY, RHINO

A twin-engine tactical fighter, the F-4 Phantom II has folding wings for easy aircraft storage and handling. The F-4C has larger wheels and brakes, cartridge starters, dual controls, boom in-flight refueling, and an inertial navigation system.

The F-4D has a precise target-identification system that increases the accuracy of weapons delivery. The F-4E has an extra fuel tank and leading-edge slats for maneuverability. A TV camera provides long-range identification of airborne and ground targets. The F-4E acquires, tracks, and designates ground targets for laser, infrared, and

electro-optically guided weapons, day or night, in any weather. The F-4G seeks enemy radar-directed anti-aircraft and surface-to-air missile sites.

Primary function: tactical fighter-bomber, reconnaissance aircraft, and interceptor
Prime contractor: McDonnell Aircraft Company, McDonnell Douglas Corporation
Power plant: F-4C/D—two General Electric J79-GE-15 turbojet engines, 17,000 thrust each; F-4E/G—two General Electric J79-GE-17 turbojet engines, 17,900 pounds thrust each
Dimensions: wingspan 38 feet 11 inches; length F-4C/D—58 feet 3 inches, F-4E/G—62 feet 11 inches; height 16 feet 5 inches
Speed: Mach 2
Ceiling: above 60,000 feet
Range: beyond 1,300 miles
Armament: F-4C/D—four AIM-7E Sparrow and four AIM-9 Sidewinder missiles, provisions for 20 mm gun pods at fuselage centerline station or outboard pylons, one fuselage centerline bomb rack and four pylon bomb racks, nuclear weapon capability; F-4E—same as F-4C/D except four AIM-7 Sparrow missiles and an additional 20 mm M61A-1 multibarrel internal gun; F-4G—same as F-4E except gun removed, and Shrike, standard ARM and HARM capability added
Maximum takeoff weight: 58,000 pounds
Crew: two—pilot, weapons systems operator

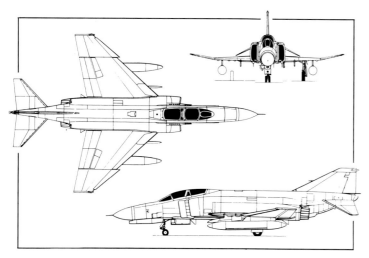

F-15 EAGLE

The F-15 is a highly maneuverable all-weather tactical fighter designed with a better than 1:1 thrust-to-weight ratio. An excellent dogfighter, its versatile weapons and flight control systems allow the pilot to handle both air-to-air combat and air-to-surface attack missions.

The F-15's pulse-Doppler radar system feeds target information into a central digital computer for effective weapons delivery. A

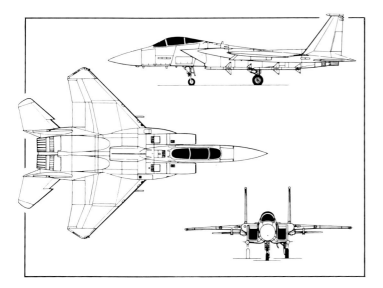

head-up display, visible in any light, projects information at eye level on the windscreen, allowing the pilot to track and destroy aircraft without looking down at the cockpit instruments. A tactical electronic system provides threat warning and automatic countermeasures.

Primary function: tactical fighter
Prime contractor: McDonnell Aircraft Company, McDonnell Douglas Corporation
Power plant: two Pratt & Whitney F-100-PW-100 turbofan engines, 25,000 pounds thrust each
Dimensions: wingspan 42 feet 10 inches, length 63 feet 9 inches, height 18 feet 7 inches
Speed: Mach 2.5
Combat ceiling: 65,000 feet
Range: ferry range 3,450 miles with conformal fuel tanks and three external fuel tanks
Armament: one M-61A1 20 mm multibarrel gun mounted internally with 940 rounds of ammunition, four AIM-9L/M Sidewinder and four AIM-7F/M Sparrow missiles, and 15,000 pounds mixed ordnance carried externally
Maximum takeoff weight: 68,000 pounds
Crew: F-15A—one—pilot, F-15B—two—pilot, student pilot

KC-10 EXTENDER

The KC-10 Extender, derived from the civilian DC-10, is an advanced tanker-cargo aircraft providing U.S. forces with increased global mobility. While performing its primary mission of aerial refueling, the KC-10 can transport 75 people and approximately 170,000 pounds of cargo. In this dual role, it has a range of about 4,400 miles. The

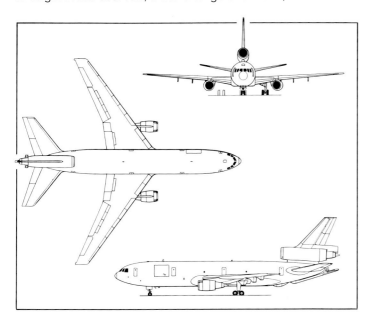

aircraft is equipped with special lighting to aid in night-time refueling.

The KC-10 boom operator, who sits in the rear of the aircraft and observes the receiving craft through a viewing window, carries out refueling operations using a digital, "fly-by-wire" control system similar to the controls in the F-16 fighter. During boom refueling operations, fuel is transferred to receiver aircraft at a rate of 1,500 gallons per minute. The drogue rate is 600 gallons per minute.

The KC-10 uses the worldwide support system of its civilian counterpart, the McDonnell Douglas DC-10 cargo plane. Most major maintenance can be taken care of at commercial facilities, leaving only routine and flight line maintenance to be completed by military personnel. This procedure makes it easier and less expensive to repair the KC-10 overseas.

Primary function: aerial refueling and transport
Prime contractor: Douglas Aircraft Company, McDonnell Douglas Corporation
Power plant: three General Electric CF6-50C2 turbofan engines, 52,500 pounds thrust each
Dimensions: wingspan 165 feet 3 inches, length 181 feet 6 inches, height 57 feet 7 inches
Speed: 550 mph
Ceiling: 42,000 feet
Range: unrefueled 11,500 miles
Maximum takeoff weight: 590,000 pounds
Crew: four—pilot, copilot, flight engineer, boom operator

C-141 STARLIFTER

The C-141's cruise speed, transoceanic range, cargo capacity, short takeoff and landing capability, and mechanized on- and off-loading have reduced cost and delivery time for airlift missions. The C-141 can carry up to 70,000 pounds of cargo nonstop for 3,500 miles.

The C-141 is the first aircraft designed to be compatible with the 463L Materiel Handling System, which permits off-loading 68,000 pounds of cargo, refueling, and reloading in less than one hour. The aircraft's cargo compartment can be easily modified to accommodate approximately 30 different missions. About 150 troops or 123 fully equipped paratroops can sit in rear-facing airline seats or side-facing canvas seats. Rollers in the aircraft floor allow quick and easy cargo pallet loading. The rollers can be turned over, providing a flat surface for loading vehicles. The C-141 can carry about 80 litter patients or 120 ambulatory patients.

The C-141 can be modified to carry the Minuteman Intercontinental Ballistic Missile and intraformation positioning sets that enable a flight of 2 to 36 aircraft to maintain formation regardless of visibility. The C-141B has in-flight refueling capability and a lengthened fuselage that increases cargo capacity by 30 percent.

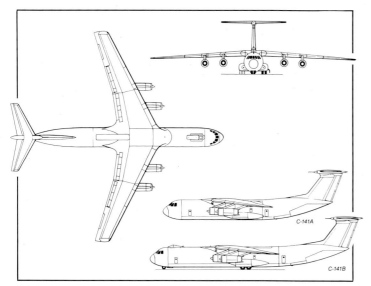

Primary function: long-range troop and cargo airlift
Prime contractor: Lockheed-Georgia Company
Power plant: four Pratt & Whitney TF33-P-7 turbofan engines, 21,000 pounds thrust each
Dimensions: wingspan 159 feet 11 inches, length 145 feet, height 39 feet 3 inches
Speed: 571 mph
Ceiling: 41,000 feet at cruising speed
Range: 3,500 miles with 70,000 pounds cargo
Maximum takeoff weight: 323,000 pounds
Crew: five—pilot, copilot, loadmaster, two flight engineers

KA-3 SKYWARRIOR
NICKNAME: WHALE

The KA-3 is a tanker adaptation of the A-3, a powerful twin-engine aircraft capable of high-altitude, high-speed attack as well as low-level attack and mine emplacement. The aircraft was originally designed as a carrier-based attack bomber that could carry large bombs, including the early A bomb.

The design of the A-3 has been adapted for a number of purposes, including photo reconnaissance, electronic countermeasures, and training.

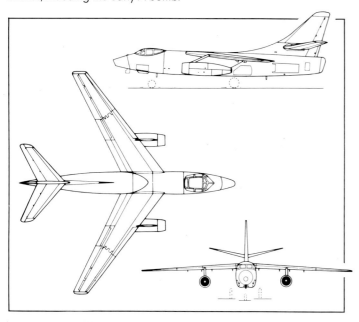

Primary function: aerial refueling
Prime contractor: Douglas Aircraft Company, McDonnell Douglas Corporation
Power plant: two Pratt & Whitney J-57 engines, 10,500 pounds thrust each
Dimensions: wingspan 72 feet 5 inches, length 75 feet 7 inches, height 22 feet 8 inches
Speed: 621 mph
Ceiling: 37,000 feet
Range: 2,300 miles
Maximum takeoff weight: 78,000 pounds
Crew: three—pilot, flight engineer, crew chief

KC-135 STRATOTANKER

A military version of the Boeing 707 passenger plane, the KC-135 replaced the KC-97, a propeller-driven tanker which could not meet the performance requirements of the increasing number of jet bombers and fighters it supported. The KC-135's primary job is refueling long-range bombers, and its work altitude of 40,000 feet and cruising speed of 530 mph more nearly match the performance of the other jet aircraft it refuels.

All internal fuel, except 1,200 gallons, can be pumped through the flying boom, the KC-135's primary method of transfer. A deck above the refueling gear can carry both passengers and cargo loads of up to 83,000 pounds.

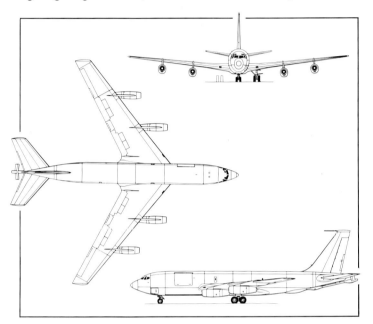

Primary function: aerial refueling
Prime contractor: The Boeing Company
Power plant: four Pratt & Whitney J-57-P-59W turbojet engines, 13,750 pounds thrust each
Dimensions: wingspan 130 feet 10 inches, length 136 feet 3 inches, height 38 feet 4 inches
Speed: 530 mph
Ceiling: 50,000 feet
Range: 1,150 miles with 120,000 pounds of transfer fuel, ferry mission 9,200 miles
Maximum takeoff weight: 297,000 pounds
Crew: four—pilot, copilot, navigator, boom operator

C-5 GALAXY
NICKNAME: FAT ALBERT, THE PICKLE

The C-5 Galaxy is a heavy-cargo transport designed to provide massive strategic airlift for deployment and supply of combat and support forces. It can carry cargo at intercontinental ranges and jet speeds and taxi on substandard surfaces during emergency operations.

With its strategic airlift partner, the C-141, which carries personnel and less bulky, lighter cargo, the C-5 can transport fully equipped, combat-ready divisions anywhere in the world. "Kneeling" landing gear lowers the cargo floor to truckbed height; a visor nose and rear door allow simultaneous loading and unloading.

The C-5 can take off fully loaded within 12,000 feet and land within 4,900 feet. Its massive weight is distributed on high-flotation landing gear with 28 wheels. The C-5's 12 integral-wing fuel tanks have a 49,000-gallon capacity—enough to fill more than six railroad tank cars. A triple inertial navigation system enables the aircraft to operate without the aid of ground-based navigational equipment.

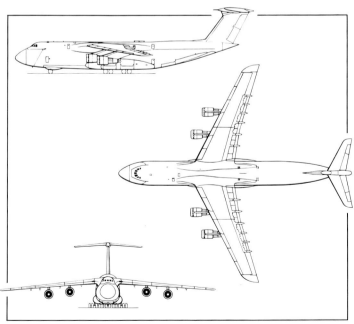

Primary function: long-range, heavy logistics transport
Prime contractor: Lockheed-Georgia Company
Power plant: four General Electric TF39-GE-1 turbofan engines, 40,100 pounds thrust each
Dimensions: wingspan 222 feet 9 inches, length 247 feet 10 inches, height 65 feet 1 inch, cargo compartment—height 13 feet 6 inches, width 19 feet
Speed: fully loaded more than 571 mph
Ceiling: 34,000 feet with 615,000 pounds weight
Range: 5,930 miles with 112,600 pounds cargo
Maximum takeoff weight: 769,000 pounds
Crew: seven to eight—pilot, copilot, navigator, flight engineers, loadmasters

C-130 HERCULES
NICKNAME: HERKY BIRD, HERK

A medium-lift aircraft designed primarily for the transport of cargo and personnel, the C-130 can be modified for other missions, including weather reconnaissance, rescue and recovery, and close air support.

The C-130 can carry six cargo pallets loaded onto the aircraft through the main loading door and ramp in the rear of the aircraft.

Rollers in the floor of the cargo bay allow efficient handling of pallets. Capable of carrying more than 42,000 pounds of cargo, the interior of the C-130 can also be adapted to carry 92 combat troops or 64 paratroops. The WC-130 modification can penetrate hurricanes and typhoons and collect data on air temperature, barometric pressure, humidity, intensity, size, and movement of storms for advance warning.

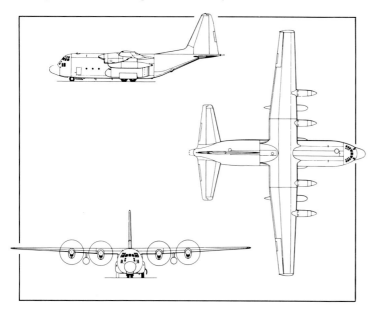

Primary function: transport, weather reconnaissance, close air support
Prime contractor: Lockheed-Georgia Company
Power plant: four Allison T56-A-15 engines, 4,000 shaft horsepower each
Dimensions: wingspan 132 feet 7 inches, length 97 feet 9 inches, height 38 feet 3 inches
Speed: 386 mph
Ceiling: above 25,000 feet
Range: 2,500 miles with 25,000 pounds of cargo
Maximum takeoff weight: 155,000 pounds
Crew: five—two pilots, navigator, flight engineer, loadmaster

P-3 ORION

The P-3 is a land-based, turbo-prop antisubmarine aircraft with a directional frequency and ranging (DIFAR) buoy, a magnetic anomaly detection (MAD) system, and advanced sensors for identifying and tracking high-performance submarines.

A digital on-board computer system rapidly retrieves, displays, and sends electronic, magnetic, and sonic data, eliminating log keeping so a crew can spend more time analyzing incoming information.

The computer automatically monitors and launches antisubmarine ordnance, which can be stored both internally and on wing pylons.

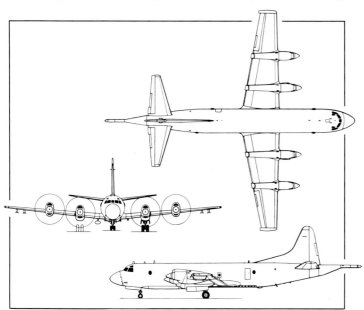

Primary function: detect, identify, track, and destroy high-performance submarines
Prime contractor: Lockheed-California Company
Power plant: four Allison T56-A14 turboshaft engines, 4,910 shaft horsepower each
Dimensions: wingspan 99 feet 8 inches, length 116 feet 10 inches, height 33 feet 8 inches
Speed: 473 mph
Ceiling: 28,300 feet
Range: 1,550 miles
Armament: MK-46 torpedoes, Bullpup air-to-ground missile, Harpoon (AGM 84) cruise missile, sonobuoys
Maximum takeoff weight: 135,000 pounds
Crew: twelve—three pilots, two flight engineers, navigator/radio operator, tactical coordinator, three sensor operators, flight technician, ordnance officer

E-2 HAWKEYE
NICKNAME: HUMMER

The E-2 Hawkeye is an all-weather, carrier-based, tactical airborne warning and control system platform. Other missions include surface surveillance coordination, strike and intercept control, search and rescue coordination, and communications relay.

The E-2 is an integral part of the carrier air wing. Its configuration includes three primary sensors: radar, IFF (Identification Friend or Foe), and a passive detection system. These are integrated with a general purpose computer which enables the E-2 to coordinate early warning, threat analyses, and countermeasures against air and surface targets.

The E-2 radar system can maintain more than 600 tracks over land and water and can detect airborne targets anywhere within a three million cubic mile surveillance envelope. An E-2 flying over New York, for example, can track all air traffic in the congested Boston-to-Washington air corridor.

Primary function: all-weather airborne early warning, command, and control functions for the carrier battle group
Prime contractor: Grumman Aerospace Corporation
Power plant: two Allison T-56-A422 turboprop engines, 4,591 shaft horsepower each
Dimensions: wingspan 80 feet 8 inches, length 57 feet 6 inches, height 18 feet 3 inches
Speed: 374 mph
Ceiling: 30,800 feet
Range: 1,400 miles
Maximum takeoff weight: 52,500 pounds
Crew: five or six—pilot, copilot, combat information center operator, weapons operator, air control operator, radar operator

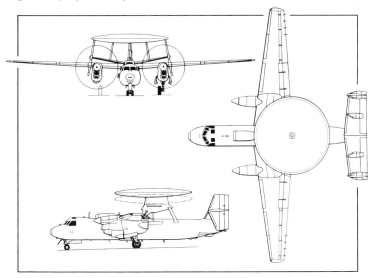

UH-1 IROQUOIS
NICKNAME: HUEY

The UH-1 is a general purpose helicopter that was widely used in Vietnam. More military and commercial models have been built of this helicopter than any other. Designed to meet standards for reliability and relatively simple field maintenance, it has been adapted to a number of missions including troop transport, medical evacuation, minefield emplacement, electronic warfare, command and control, and instrument training.

The UH-1 can accommodate 11-14 troops, a medic and six patients on litters, or 3,880 pounds of cargo.

Primary function: general purpose light helicopter
Prime contractor: Bell Helicopter Textron
Power plant: one Allison 250-C20 turboshaft engine with 400 horsepower
Dimensions: diameter of main rotor 48 feet, length of fuselage 41 feet 11 inches, height 14 feet 6 inches
Speed: 127 mph
Ceiling: 12,600 feet
Range: 318 miles
Maximum takeoff weight: 9,500 pounds
Crew: three—pilot, copilot, crew chief

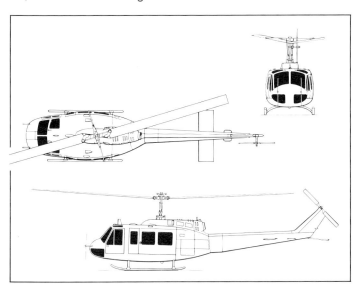

HH-3 JOLLY GREEN GIANT

The HH-3 is a land- and water-based helicopter that has been used both for search and rescue of troops and in contingency plans for astronaut recovery.

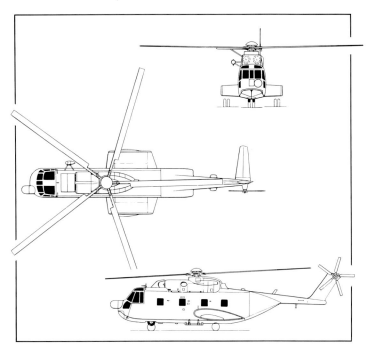

Protected in combat by armor plating, internal self-sealing fuel tanks, dispensable fuel tanks, and a high-speed rescue hoist with 240 feet of cable, the HH-3 was widely used to recover downed aircrews during the Vietnam war. Some models have also been equipped for midair retrieval of aerospace hardware.

The HH-3 can accommodate 25 equipped troops, 15 patients on litters, or 5,000 pounds of cargo. It has a rear ramp for straight-in loading.

Primary function: transport, combat search and rescue
Prime contractor: Sikorsky Aircraft Division, United Technologies Corporation
Power plant: two General Electric T58-GE-5 turboshaft engines, 1,500 horsepower each
Dimensions: diameter of main rotor 62 feet, length of fuselage 57 feet 3 inches, height overall 18 feet 1 inch
Speed: 166 mph
Ceiling: 11,100 feet
Range: 465 miles
Armament: two 7.62 mm machine guns
Maximum takeoff weight: 22,050 pounds
Crew: two—pilot, copilot, with provision for flight engineer

CH-47 CHINOOK

An all-weather helicopter, the CH-47's missions include movement of repair parts, ammunition, and fuel as well as the tactical transfer of troops, artillery, and special weapons on the battlefield.

As many as 44 troops or 24 litters and 2 attendants can be accommodated in the main cabin. The CH-47 can carry a full artillery section including troops and ammunition. The rear loading ramp can be left completely open to allow transport and parachute or free drop of extra-long cargo loads; a 28,000-pound load can be carried on an external hook.

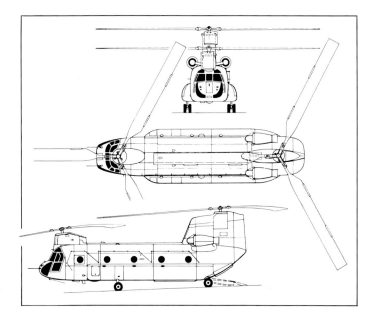

Primary function: transfer of fuel, ammunition, repair parts, and tactical movement of artillery and troops
Prime contractor: Boeing Vertol and Agusta
Power plant: two Lycoming T55-L-11C turboshaft engines, 3,750 horsepower each
Dimensions: diameter of rotors 60 feet, length of fuselage 51 feet, height to top of rear rotor hub 18 feet 7 inches
Speed: 189 mph
Ceiling: 15,000 feet
Combat radius: 115 miles
Maximum takeoff weight: 33,000 pounds
Crew: three—two pilots and crew chief or commander

AH-64 APACHE

The AH-64 is capable of destroying armored tanks in all weather conditions and at night, and of supporting troops at front lines.

A target acquisition designation sight (TADS) includes forward-looking infrared (FLIR), direct-viewing optics, a laser rangefinder and tracker, and TV. A pilot night-vision sensor (PNVS) is an advanced FLIR system. The TADS and PNVS systems enable the crew to target tanks accurately with a Hellfire laser-guided missile. Crew areas are protected with boron armor shields that can withstand 23 mm ammunition hits.

Primary function: attack of armored tanks
Prime contractor: McDonnell Douglas Helicopter Company, McDonnell Douglas Corporation
Power plant: two GE T700-GE-701 turboshaft engines, 1,696 horsepower each
Dimensions: main rotor diameter 48 feet, length overall with rotors turning 58 feet 3 inches, height overall 15 feet 3 inches
Speed: 192 mph
Ceiling: 21,000 feet
Combat radius: 300 miles with internal fuel
Armament: 30 mm automatic cannon, 16 Hellfire or TOW (tube-launched, optically tracked, wire-guided) missiles, 76 FFAR (folding-fin aerial rockets)
Maximum takeoff weight: 21,000 pounds
Crew: two — pilot, copilot/gunner

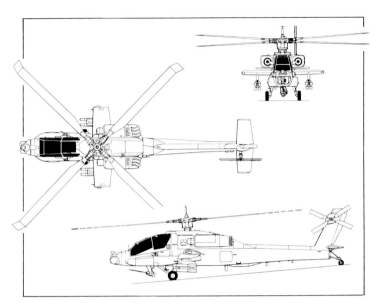

UH-60 BLACK HAWK

Designed primarily for air assault and rescue, the UH-60 can quickly transport an entire 11-man, fully equipped squad in high altitudes and high temperatures. A large cabin can be used for reconnaissance, medical evacuation, and the resupply of troops. The aircraft can improve an Army division's mobility by repositioning a crew of six, a 105 mm howitzer, and up to 30 rounds of ammunition in a single lift. Its cargo hook lifts 8,000 pounds externally.

Armored or redundant parts and systems enable the UH-60 to survive repeated small arms hits. Its airframe is designed to absorb the shock of a crash, deforming on impact to protect the crew. The Black Hawk's full squad-carrying capacity significantly improves the small unit's ability to retain control under combat landing conditions and permits more rapid replacement of ammunition and other supplies in the field.

Primary function: attack and rescue
Prime contractor: Sikorsky Aircraft Division, United Technologies Corporation
Power plant: two General Electric T700-GE-700 turboshaft engines, 1,560 horsepower each
Dimensions: main rotor diameter 53 feet 8 inches, length of fuselage 50 feet, height overall 16 feet 10 inches
Speed: 184 mph
Ceiling: 19,000 feet
Range: 373 miles
Armament: provision for Hellfire missiles and two M60 side-firing machine guns
Maximum takeoff weight: 16,260 pounds
Crew: three — two pilots, one crew chief

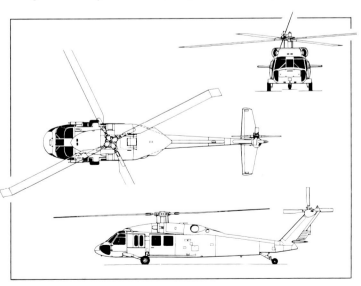

AH-1 COBRA

Pilots flew the original configuration of this attack helicopter extensively in Vietnam. Its narrow fuselage and low profile, designed for speed and efficiency, make it easy to camouflage under nets or trees. The Cobra proved very effective against lightly armored vehicles, but it could not destroy tanks until the addition of the TOW (tube-launched, optically tracked, wire-guided) missile.

The modernized AH-1S Cobra is a single-engine close support and attack helicopter capable of damaging enemy armored tanks. Its TOW missile can be aimed accurately at a range of more than two miles; its 20 mm cannon is effective against light armored vehicles.

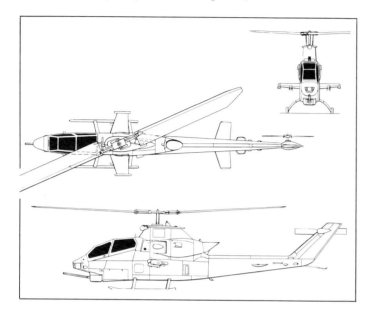

Primary function: close support and attack
Prime contractor: Bell Helicopter Textron
Power plant: one Lycoming T53-L-703 engine with 1,800 horsepower
Dimensions: diameter of main rotor 44 feet, length of fuselage 44 feet 7 inches, height overall 13 feet 8 inches
Speed: 212 mph
Ceiling: 12,200 feet
Combat radius: 315 miles
Armament: 20 mm cannon, 38 FFAR rockets, 8 TOW missiles
Maximum takeoff weight: 10,000 pounds
Crew: two—pilot, copilot/gunner

OH-6 CAYUSE
NICKNAME: LOACH

The OH-6 is a light observation helicopter that can be equipped for combat. Sound blanketing of the power plant, including intake and exhaust, makes this one of the world's quietest helicopters. The OH-6 holds a distance record of 2,213 miles from California to Florida—a nonstop flight with one pilot.

Dual controls allow either pilot or copilot to fly the aircraft. The rear cargo compartment can accommodate four equipped soldiers with seating on the floor. The OH-6 can adapt to a number of different missions, including courier runs, radio relay, traffic control, and reconnaissance.

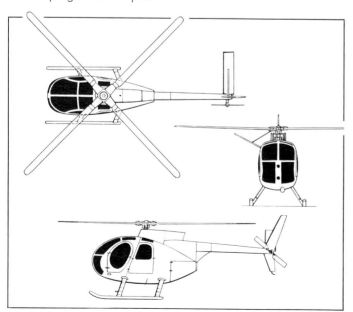

Primary function: observation
Prime contractor: Hughes Helicopter
Power plant: one Allison T63-A-5A turboshaft engine with 317 horsepower
Dimensions: diameter of main rotor 26 feet 4 inches, length of fuselage 23 feet, height to top of rotor hub 8 feet 1 inch
Speed: 150 mph
Ceiling: 15,800 feet
Range: 380 miles at 5,000 feet
Armament: provision for 7.6 mm machine gun, rockets, and/or a grenade launcher
Maximum takeoff weight: 2,550 pounds
Crew: two—pilot, copilot

CH-53A SEA STALLION

The CH-53A is a heavy-lift, twin-engine assault transport helicopter capable of operating in all weather conditions. In early flight tests, its unusual maneuverability allowed loops and rolls.

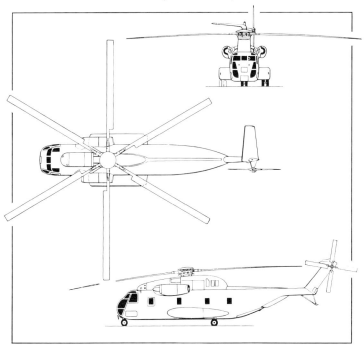

The main cabin of the CH-53A can accommodate 37 combat-equipped troops or 24 stretchers and 4 attendants. The cargo bay can hold two Hawk missiles with cable reels and controls, a 105 mm howitzer and carriage, or two Jeeps. An in-flight drop and retrieval system makes cargo transfer possible without ground support. Floor rollers, a hydraulically operated loading system, a full-size rear opening and ramp allow easy loading and unloading.

The CH-53A has a watertight hull. The main rotors and tail pylon fold for stowage aboard ship.

Primary function: movement of cargo, personnel, and damaged aircraft
Prime contractor: Sikorsky Aircraft Division, United Technologies Corporation
Power plant: two General Electric T64-GE-6 turboshaft engines, 2,850 horsepower each
Dimensions: diameter of main rotor 72 feet 3 inches, length of fuselage 72 feet 3 inches, height 24 feet 11 inches
Speed: 173 mph
Ceiling: 21,000 feet
Range: 257 miles
Maximum takeoff weight: 42,000 pounds
Crew: three—pilot, copilot, crew chief/loadmaster

Naval Reserve F-14 on USS Ranger

Naval Reserve F-14
Tomcats